W9-DEI-260

GEORGE RUSSELL (AE)	Richard M. Kain and James H. O'Brien
IRIS MURDOCH	Donna Gerstenberger
MARY LAVIN	Zack Bowen
FRANK O'CONNOR	James H. Matthews
ELIZABETH BOWEN	Edwin J. Kenney, Jr.
WILLIAM ALLINGHAM	Alan Warner
SEAMUS HEANEY	Robert Buttel
THOMAS DAVIS	Eileen Sullivan

CHARLES ROBERT MATURIN

Robert E. Lougy

Lewisburg
BUCKNELL UNIVERSITY PRESS
London: ASSOCIATED UNIVERSITY PRESSES

Associated University Presses, Inc.
Cranbury, New Jersey 08512

Associated University Presses
108 New Bond Street
London W1Y OQX, England

Library of Congress Cataloging in Publication Data

Lougy, Robert E
Charles Robert Maturin.

(Irish writers series)
Bibliography: p.
1. Maturin, Charles Robert, 1780–1824.
PR4987.M7Z77 823'.7 [B] 75-168813
ISBN 0-8387-7941-7
ISBN 0-8387-7986-7 (pbk.)

For Gwenda

The author gratefully acknowledges the kind permission of the Regents of the University of Texas to quote from *The Correspondence of Sir Walter Scott and Charles Robert Maturin*.

PRINTED IN THE UNITED STATES OF AMERICA

Contents

Chronology

1780 Born on September 25. Son of William and Fidelia Maturin. One of six children.

1795 Enters Trinity College in Dublin. Member of Historical Society and winner of a scholarship and several prizes for poetry.

1800 Graduates from Trinity College.

1803 Ordained as a minister.

1804 Appointed to the curacy of Loughrea. Married Henrietta Kingsberry on October 7. Was in Loughrea for only about a year when he obtained the curacy of St. Peters in Dublin, where he remained until his death.

1807 Published at his own expense *The Family of Montorio* under the pseudonym of Dennis Jasper Murphy.

1808 Published, again at his own expense, *The Wild Irish Boy*.

1809 William Maturin is dismissed from his government position.

1812 Published *The Milesian Chief*. Also began a correspondence with Sir Walter Scott that continued until Maturin's death.

1816 Maturin's first drama, *Bertram; or the Castle of St. Aldobrand,* was produced at Drury Lane.

1817 Maturin's second drama, *Manuel,* was produced at the Drury Lane Theatre.

1818 *Women; or Pour et Contre* published.

1819 *Fredolfo,* Maturin's third and last drama, produced in Covent Garden.

1820 *Melmoth the Wanderer* published.

1821 *The Universe, a poem,* published. Its authorship was disputed.

1824 *The Albigenses* published. Maturin died on October 30.

Charles Robert Maturin

1

The Early Years, 1780–1815

Charles Robert Maturin was born in 1780 into very comfortable and promising circumstances and died forty-four years later, wracked and beaten by poverty and disappointment. Maturin was temperamentally, constitutionally, and perhaps even intellectually unable to fit into the role of gentleman-clergyman that his ancestors had prominently played and that his father had persuaded him to assume. Had he been independently wealthy, his later eccentricities and strange tastes would most likely have been accepted as the oddities of a rich artist; but as it was, his mannerisms when combined with the fact that he wrote fiction and drama containing less than orthodox Christian views were enough to prevent him from gaining preferment within the Church. Critics, and churchmen as well, were often guilty of attributing the viewpoints and beliefs of his characters to himself, perhaps because Maturin often seems to be of the devil's party. Consequently, it is in his "worst" characters that one often finds Maturin at his best. But it was not only the nature of Maturin's writings that prevented his rise within the Church. In the past, the Church of England has been fairly tolerant of its literary clergymen and it is more probable that the real causes of Maturin's dissatisfaction are to be found in his temperament. He entered the Church to gain security and prestige, and he was unable to assume the mask of conformity and orthodoxy that might have led to advancement.

Maturin had graduated from Trinity College in 1800, having achieved honors as a classical scholar and for his "rhetorical and poetical productions," was ordained three years later, and became the curate of a small and remote church in Loughrea. During an otherwise dismal year there, he met and married a beautiful and talented young woman, also from an ecclesiastical family, Miss Henrietta Kingsberry. Through the influences of his family, he obtained the curacy of St. Peter's in Dublin, and there he remained until his death in 1824. Although the curacy was in the midst of a wealthy and prestigious neighborhood, Maturin's pay was not commensurate, and so he and his family moved into his father's house in order to stretch his rather meager stipend. But despite the smallness of his salary and the rapid increase in the size of his family, Maturin was able to publish *The Family of Montorio* in 1807 out of his own pocket. In 1809, however, Maturin's father suddenly fell from favor, being charged by the government with fraud, and a much greater financial burden fell upon Maturin's own shoulders. True poverty, from which he was never to rise, descended upon him.

One of Maturin's contemporary biographers speaks of a deep-seated conflict within him: "In that situation [the curacy of St. Peters] he remained—a clergyman and a poet; his profession drawing him one way, his genius another—and necessity to both." There can be little doubt that Maturin was born to be a writer, but he would have preferred, if fate had given him a choice, to do his work on Mt. Parnassus rather than in Grub Street.

There is a certain quality of the "dandy" about Maturin; several writers of the time commented on the contrast between the author they had expected to find—like his novels, gloomy, forbidding and melancholy—and the man they found—"the gayest of the gay, passionately fond of society. . . ." Yet, at the same time, several also make mention of his countenance, which, at unguarded moments, revealed "the profoundest melancholy." His manner of dressing, the myths that he not only allowed, but encouraged to develop about himself, and his self-conscious eccentricities of behavior all suggest an attempt to shield himself against the destructive effects of poverty and against the disparity between his once high expectations and the starkness of his actual circumstances. He, like the aesthetes of the late nineteenth century, created a literature and a style of life that served to muffle, albeit not wholly effectively, the discord of his daily existence.

Maturin had read and assimilated the earlier gothic novels, especially those of Mrs. Radcliffe and Gregory "Monk" Lewis, known for his classic exercise in horror, *The Monk*, and by the time of his father's ruin in 1809, he had already published two novels at his own expense. This fact somewhat reduces the plausibility of the suggestion that he originally turned to the gothic novel because he felt it to have greater commercial possibilities. It is more likely that he chose the gothic novel because its scope coincided with both his interests and his talents and gave him the opportunity to explore areas of human experience possibly less suited to other genres. In his first novel, Maturin's style and techniques are somewhat derivative; but even in *The Family of Montorio* (published under the pseudonym of Dennis Jasper Murphy and subtitled *The Fatal Revenge*), Maturin is discovering those themes that he will explore throughout his writings—fear, guilt, and the "midnight darkness of the soul."

For *Montorio* Maturin chooses a setting and a time that provide a rich background for the novel's plot. The story is set in Italy during the last part of the seventeenth century and revolves around the Montorio family, an illustrious and ancient family of Naples. The plot line of the novel is among Maturin's more intricate, involving the devious and complex machinations of Count Orazio to revenge himself upon his younger brother for a treachery the brother had committed more than twenty years before the action of the novel begins. Dedicated to revenge himself upon his brother for cheating him out of his inheritance, Orazio journeys to the East where he becomes versed in the occult and supernatural, and then he returns to Italy, disguised as a monk and using the name of Father Schemoli. He manages to become the confessor of his younger brother, who has become a fervent devotee. Schemoli plans to exploit the family's fascination with the supernatural to gain power over his brother's sons, Annibal and Ippolito, and to force them to kill their father. The rest of the novel, filled with missing bodies, subterranean passages, wandering ghosts, spectres, and concealed corpses, unfolds the methods and means he uses to achieve his revenge. However, his revenge is unexpectedly made very bitter when his brother, just before dying, tells him that Annibal and Ippolito are in fact Orazio's own sons, whom he had believed killed by the brother. The agony caused by this revelation kills Orazio, the sons flee to become soldiers and are soon both killed, and the novel concludes moralistically that:

> He who sought vengeance as atrocious as the crime that provoked it, finds it poured out on his own children; and they who desired the knowledge of things concealed from man, found pursuit accompanied by guilt, and terminated by misery and punishment.

The plot is one of the weaker aspects of *The Family of Montorio*. Maturin devotes two of the three volumes to developing the figure of Father Schemoli as a supernatural being, in commerce with diabolic agents and capable of transcending both space and time, and then in the third volume, attempts a naturalistic account of the deeds and powers he possesses. As critics of the time pointed out, it is inconceivable that a mere man could be in so many places at exactly the right time and wield such psychological and physical power as Father Schemoli; but by the third volume we have already accepted him in these terms and feel somewhat deceived when Maturin tries to explain away all of these superhuman qualities. In his later works, such as *Bertram* and *Melmoth,* Maturin allows the supernatural to remain unencumbered by rational and quasi-scientific explanations. But as a young clergyman writing his first novel,

Maturin understandably did not want to stretch the unorthodox in the work any more than necessary.

The Family of Montorio is, when compared to works such as *Women* and *Melmoth*, clearly inferior in terms of design and conception of character; but it contains some powerful and imaginative writing, suggesting Maturin's latent genius, and also possesses most of the major themes that were to occupy Maturin throughout his literary career. Within it we also see how well acquainted Maturin was with the nature of the gothic world and the gothic landscape, where nothing ever happened gratuitously. The gothic universe is a theocentric one, an animistic version of the early eighteenth century world-view, which saw all earthly phenomena as manifestations of a divinely conceived and somewhat mechanistically ordered cosmos. Throughout the gothic novel—but especially toward the conclusion—we realize that the characters within it operate not as free and independent entities, but as objects of a larger and more powerful force that can be either malignant or ultimately just and benign, as for example in *Montorio* when we see "the dispensation of a higher hand . . . visible to the most weak and limited eye."

One of the recurrent concerns in Maturin's fiction is the extent and strength of man's free will, both in resisting the external forces of evil, as embodied by figures such as Father Schemoli and Melmoth, and also in resisting those forces of evil that every man contains within himself. These forces are stronger than reason and represent the latent possibility within a man's soul of committing deeds of which he believes himself incapable. Maturin describes this aspect of man metaphorically:

> When a man exhibits his mind, he shows you a city, whose public walks and palaces are ostentatiously displayed, while its prisons, its cages of unclean birds, its hold of foul and hidden evil are concealed; or he exhibits it as he would the sovereign of that city, when he stands on the pinnacle of his pride, and looks round on the ample prospect of his own magnificence, not as when he flies from the resort of man, and herds with the beasts; when his power is lost in degradation, and his form buried in brutality.

The landscape of *The Family of Montorio* is primarily psychological, one structured to enhance the moods of terror, fear, and suspense. There is only a perfunctory attempt to depict topography realistically. There exists, in fact, a disproportionate relationship between the number of words expended to define the terrain and the imprecise and vague notion we have of it. But the landscape is for the most part an externalization of the inner conflict of the characters. It also functions—at times, in an almost mechanical fashion—to further advance and heighten the plot: oceans exist for the purpose of creating tidal waves and storms, mountains for showing the disastrous consequences of earthquakes, and rivers for flooding and for carrying the characters from one place to another.

Like the physical landscape, the psychological landscape—of which the former is often but a projection—is also of a circumscribed nature. Certain emotions such as laughter, light wit, tranquility, and simple contentment are outside such a world; emotions, like the violent natural elements, must themselves be strong, violent, and rending. Consequently, the dialogue becomes the vehicle of emotions of fear, passionate hate, equally passionate (though often passionless) love, and heart-breaking sorrow. People never just talk—they plead, coerce, bribe, threaten, adore, whisper, intimidate. In a novel filled with many strengths and the promise of even better writing to come, it is with dialogue that Maturin has the most trouble, especially when he is trying to convey the more tender emotions. In dialogue conveying hate, fear, contempt, Maturin is much stronger. Probably because of his own recognition of the often stilted quality of his dialogue, Maturin presents the bulk of *Montorio* in the form of letters, diaries, and manuscripts.

In contrast to the lame prose we find in some of his dialogues, when he is describing the emotions of horror and fear and the realm of the unknown and supernatural that give rise to these emotions, his language is strong, fast-moving and imaginative. As Maturin said in his preface to *The Milesian Chief* "If I possess any talent it is that of darkening the gloomy, and of deepening the sad; of painting life in extreme, and representing those struggles of passion when the soul trembles on the verge of the unlawful and the unhallowed."

One of the most vividly realized passages in the novel is that in which Father Schemoli tells Annibal that he, Father Schemoli, is the spirit of a man who has been dead for over twenty years. During his description of "death" and the descent into hell, we see evidence of an imaginative genius in Maturin, beside which the best that Radcliffe and Walpole can offer grows pale by comparison:

> In the heart of the fire, lay a human body, unconsumed for two thousand years; for they had but partially raised it for

> some magic purpose, when they were destroyed. . . . But now they were compelled by a stronger power than their own . . . to waken from that sleep of horrid existence, to renew the unfinished spell, and to raise the corpse that lay in the flames. It was a sight of horror, even for an unblessed soul to see them. Rent from the smoking rocks, that they wished might fall on them, and hide them; their forms of metallic and rocky cinder, where the human feature horribly struggled through burnt and blackening masses, discoloured with the calcined and dingy hues of fire, purple, and red, and green; their stony eyes rolling with strange life; their sealed jaws rent open by sounds, that were like the rush of subterrene winds. . . .

Irish literature had to wait for more than a hundred years, until Joyce's *Portrait of the Artist as a Young Man,* before another writer would equal in vividness and grotesqueness Maturin's imaginative rendering of the horrors of Hell. Although Walter Scott in his 1810 review of *Montorio* did not approve of the genre Maturin used as a vehicle for his powers, he recognized, probably in passages such as those cited above, the real powers that the young author possessed:

> We have at no time more earnestly desired to extend our voice to a bewildered traveller, than towards this young man, whose taste is so inferior to his powers of imagination and expression, that we never saw a more remarkable instance of genius degraded by the labour in which it is employed.

In his first novel Maturin tentatively develops several motifs that become the major focal points of his later work. The first, for which he is perhaps most famous, is the theme of the Wandering Jew, the man separated either because of a great crime or great guilt from the rest of mankind. Lord Byron's *Childe Harold's Pilgrimage* was not published until 1812; but in 1807, Maturin was already experimenting with the conception of such a figure and had undoubtedly read Coleridge's *The Rime of the Ancient Mariner*, which depicts the archetypal lonely man endowed with great power, but cursed with a suffering that he is powerless to allay. Not until *Melmoth* in 1820 does Maturin elevate such a figure into the realm of myth and symbol, but in *Montorio* he clearly has the possibilities of such a character in mind, for Father Schemoli himself is the classic example of such a figure, a predecessor of Melmoth the Wanderer. And as in the case of Melmoth, we see in Schemoli Maturin's wedding together of two legends, that of the Wandering Jew and that of Faust—a man cut off and elevated above mankind by virtue of a knowledge forbidden to ordinary men, a knowledge that is the source of his great power, his great suffering, and his violent end. But Maturin also provides an ironic twist to these legends in that Schemoli and Melmoth are destroyed as much by ignorance as by excessive knowledge.

The final motif in *Montorio* is that of sexual repression and sublimation manifested in religious fanaticism, in erotic fanaticism, and in an excessively idealized concept of love. Such fanaticism, as Maturin sees it, results in cruelty and aggression, directed either toward others or toward oneself. This motif is the major theme of *Women: or Pour et Contre* and is significant in both *Melmoth* and Maturin's last novel, *The Albigenses*. As an Anglican minister, Maturin shared with others a fear of the Roman Catholic Church, viewing it as a bulwark of the reactionary political forces of the time. It is in part for this reason that his explorations of religious fanaticism often center on it; but in *Women: or Pour et Contre*, he is equally critical of Calvinistic Evangelicalism. In much of his fiction, women especially are victimized by a religious and social code that demands sexual repression since they, unlike men, did not have access to harlots and brothels for release of sexual passions. It is more than coincidental that several of Maturin's central male characters, for example Ippolito in *Montorio* and Ormsby Bethel in *The Wild Irish Boy,* find their way to gaming-houses or brothels during times of emotional anguish or turmoil. A good part of *Montorio* is devoted to the journal of a young woman, Rosolia di Valozzi, which is a fascinating study of the agonies of a young woman who discovers that the desires of her body and the nature of her dreams do not correspond to the idea of Love she has been taught. In her attempts to deny or repress these "wayward" feelings, she tries to divert her passions into a love for God and nature, and thus her religious poetry and descriptions of Nature consequently assume erotic overtones.

Maturin's next novel, *The Wild Irish Boy*, was also published at his own expense the year after *Montorio* appeared. But unlike *Montorio*, this novel seems to have arisen less from Maturin's desire to explore human nature than from his wish to make money. For example, by calling it *The Wild Irish Boy*, he undoubtedly hoped to capitalize on the success that Lady Morgan's *The Wild Irish Girl* had enjoyed the previous year. Even in the preface to his second novel, Maturin makes it clear that he did not enjoy writing it and did not like it once it was written. Although Maturin is sometimes guilty of lapses in critical taste, his critical preference in this case is on the mark. That rough and crude, but powerful genius that Sir Walter Scott recognized is almost smothered here by Maturin's attempt to satisfy the public's taste.

The hero of the novel is Ormsby Bethel, a young man of mysterious background and origin who only at the end of the novel is reunited with his father. In this respect, the novel is a *Bildungsroman*, but the possibilities inherent in the story of a young man's quest for identity never materialize. Maturin rather clumsily handles the problem of point of view and never seems sure of the novel's thematic focus. The plot involves Ormsby's rather willing descent into the dissolute and immoral upper echelons of Irish society after he inherits a large sum of money from his uncle. The novel contains the stock figures of hero, villain, and seductress. It is also filled with mistaken intentions, secret identities, mysterious lovers, attempted murder, and sundry other devices to whet the reader's appetite and fulfill what Maturin assumed to be the public's expectations for the best-selling novels of the day.

But this is also the first novel where Maturin chooses Ireland and its people as his subjects, although he laments in the preface the fact that it does not deal even more with Ireland: "my heart was full of it, but I was compelled by the laws of this mode of composition to consult the pleasures of my readers, not my own." The period in which the action is set is indicated only by the observation that "there is some idea of petitioning . . .

for a repeal of the act of union; this is the time for an Irishman to make himself conspicuous, on the one side or the other . . . ," probably between 1801 and 1808. The actual date matters little, for, unlike *The Albigenses*, the historical background plays only a minor part in the novel. The only character who speaks anti-English sentiments is DeLacey, a rich, old Milesian, who is throughout the novel an admirable and noble man, but nevertheless an anachronism. He has some strong things to say about the treatment of Ireland by the English, "those who have desolated the country, and razed every mark of power or of resistance from the face of it. . . ."

Although it might seem reasonable to suppose that Maturin, an Irishman who strongly identified with Ireland's history and fate, harbored sentiments similar to those uttered by DeLacey, one has to remember that Maturin was also, of course, a Protestant minister and that he puts some glowing comments about the English in the mouth of Corbett, the novel's most favorable character, who "knew the liberal and public spirit of many of the English nobility" and that such men "were . . . intent on cultivating the morals and minds of the lower orders, and providing for the temporal and spiritual comforts of the poor. . . ." Maturin seems here to take with one hand what he has given with the other and consequently creates a kind of obsequious tone not at all flattering to himself. This may be in part due to fear of offending the very people he hoped would buy his book; but it probably also arises from the simultaneous love and hate that he, like Yeats and Joyce, seemed to feel toward Ireland. While most of his discussion of his country in this novel is of a broad and general nature, we see some evidence of this ambivalence in young Ormsby's fantasies about

> . . . some abode peopled by fair forms, human in their affection, their habits, in every thing but vice and weakness; to these I have imagined myself giving laws, and becoming their sovereign and benefactor.

But in fantasizing further, he also identifies faults:

> I imagined them possessed of the most shining qualities that can enter into the human character . . . but proud, irritable, indolent, and superstitious—burning with excellence, which because they wanted regulation, wanted both dignity and utility.

The race he imagined is, of course, the Irish.

A more interesting and important aspect of a novel that fails to face Ireland and its problems directly, is the relationship Maturin depicts between Ormsby and Lady Montrevor, a woman with a history of intrigue and romances, older than the young man, but still beautiful. Ormsby's feelings for her are not, in spite of his protestations, spiritual: "I got home on fire with emotions I did not understand. . . . I did not believe it possible seriously to love a married woman." After being with her, Ormsby writes that "I abandoned myself to the fatal indulgences of thought" and "fell into an agony of passion that almost made me incapable of reason." These passages, regardless of their stilted language, demonstrate the sexual nature of the attraction. The love of a young man for an older married woman is not so unusual, and if this were the only aspect of the relationship Maturin had developed, it would need little commentary. But not only is Lady Montrevor considerably older than Ormsby; she is also a former love of his father and will, at the novel's conclusion, become Ormsby's stepmother. In light of Maturin's first novel, in which two sons kill a man they think is their own father, this relationship becomes even more interesting as another example of Maturin skirting the edge of areas of relationships that are a repressed part of the psychic life of man. In each case, however, Maturin employs a technique corresponding closely to what Freud in his discussion of dreams and art has called "displacement"—Maturin treats the theme of the desire of the son to kill his father and to sleep with his mother; in each case, much of the underlying resonance and strength of his novels arise from the presence of these themes, but because he cannot treat these matters directly, he displaces the father in his fiction by making him an uncle and the mother by making her unrelated by blood.

There are other examples of this technique. For example, in the relationship between Cyprian and Ippolito in *Montorio,* there are strong overtones of homosexuality. At one point Ippolito, asked for a kiss by Cyprian, replies, "you do what you will with me; I have never kissed one of my own sex before; but do what you will with me." At another point when Ippolito is departing, "Cyprian felt his throat swell, and his head grow giddy; amid all his sufferings, the thought of being deserted by him he loved, had never been suggested to him; and when now it was presented to his mind, he felt as if he had never been unhappy before." Again, as in the previous examples, the language Cyprian uses and the symptoms he displays are ridden with convention, but nevertheless are Maturin's rendering of the emotion of sexual love. The fact that, at the novel's conclusion, we learn that Cyprian is really Rosolia di Valozzi in disguise does not mitigate the homosexual overtones of the relationship. It is simply another version of the technique of displacement: depict homosexual love, but displace one of the males by a female. These incidents from Maturin's first two novels are too numerous to be simply coincidental. They are deliberately created, and all deal with taboos; in each case, either the revelation of true identity or a premature death extricated Maturin from having to fulfill the terms of the experiences he has presented. The pattern of these incidents strongly corresponds to Freud's description of how we take "latent dream thought" that has been repressed in our unconscious and render it through "dream work," during which time displacement occurs, into what he calls "manifest dream content." In both the gothic and the taboo, Maturin deals with the twilight regions of human life, between waking and sleeping, between the conscious and unconscious. Both represent the demonic and the irrational, those repressed but real fascinations we feel toward horror and fear. Perhaps Maturin best defines the realms he finds most fascinating when in *Montorio* he speaks of emotions that are "like the faint feelings of pain in sleep, just vexing our dreams, and warring on the outworks of sensation."

Maturin's fascination not only with sexual taboos

but also with the diabolic, the occult, and the supernatural, was one that, for an Anglican divine, carried certain risks. And although in a literal sense, the only real danger he faced was disfavor in the eyes of the Church, another danger, less concrete but more serious, was that of continually moving further beyond that very life from which he was trying to find temporary escape. To write as Maturin did was to indulge in what is pleasurable in so far as it stands opposed to the painful reality of the present moment, no matter how horrible or grotesque the indulgence's form might be. In Maturin's case, it assumes primarily the form of exploring those aspects of human life that were far outside his ordinary circles. And as Maturin's literary career progresses, we see this cycle in operation—an ever increasing fascination that must explore deeper and deeper into the "midnight darkness of the soul," until finally one wonders whether Maturin finds himself, in a work such as *Melmoth,* pulled asunder not only from religious excesses, but from the very concept of orthodox religion, whatever its form.

This tension between Maturin's artistic vision and his clerical profession appears in much of his writing. It is, perhaps, most apparent in the incongruity that often appears between the professed moral purpose of his writings and the writings themselves—between the didactic meanings imposed by Maturin the clergyman upon a work that cannot accommodate such a meaning. His imagination and fascinations seem too strongly impelled toward those very things which, if we are to accept the moral purpose of the work, we are to shun. Although *Montorio* has such a purpose, it is expressed in fairly broad terms; however, in *The Wild Irish Boy,* the moral or didactic purpose is explicitly that "the more terrible consequences of practical deviation may be inferred and deprecated from their display." Fortunately, Maturin himself seems to have forgotten this moral purpose for the most part. The real strength of this novel is seen when Maturin moves farthest away from the conventions of the sentimental romance and allows his imagination the freedom to roam uninhibited through scenes with a strange mixture of corruption and innocence, insanity and sanity, death and sexuality, lust and religion. These scenes are purely gratuitous, having no integral relationship to the main plot line, and function, like some of Maturin's interpolated tales and poems, to give vent to an aspect of his imagination that must have felt constrained by the didactic and the sentimental.

The poor reception of *The Wild Irish Boy* must have been doubly frustrating to Maturin, because he felt he had pandered himself to the public. That he tried to put his second fictional effort out of his mind completely is suggested by his first letter to Walter Scott four years later, in which he refers to himself as "an obscure Irishman—the author only of two trifling performances, the Romance of 'Montorio' and of the 'Milesian'." He certainly had not forgotten *The Wild Irish Boy,* but he did not want to remind either Scott or himself of its existence. Meanwhile, Maturin's financial and professional position continued to deteriorate.

Maturin's father, a successful and wealthy civil servant, had raised his children to expect a life of comfort and prosperity. But in 1809, for reasons that are still unclear, the government brought forth a charge of malversation or fraud against the father. Maturin and his family were at this time residing with his parents to ease the financial strain imposed upon him by his position. Almost thirty years old, Maturin had a wife and family, very little money to support them, and not much hope of advancement. Two of his novels had already been financial disasters and now, without the support of a father who had lived up to his income, he could hardly afford to pay for the publication of any more. It is not surprising, then, that the themes of poverty and misfortune repeat themselves so often in his fiction.

In order to supplement his meager stipend, Maturin used his wife's money and took a large house in which he could board and tutor students from the College of Dublin. He undoubtedly made some money in this venture—he speaks of his annual income from teaching as fluctuating between 1000 and 500 pounds—but it is questionable how rewarding in other ways his new vocation was. Idman maintains that Maturin "was undoubtedly successful in his vocation as a teacher," and he quotes from a contemporary of Maturin who visited him during this period and wrote of his "elastic and ardent" genius. But in 1813, Maturin's enthusiasm was waning considerably, as evidenced by one of his letters to Scott:

> I found the greatest difficulty in procuring the few (students) I have, and almost equal difficulty in keeping them—it is impossible to describe the "Variety of wretchedness" attendant on this line of life—The Caprice of parents, the

> dullness of Children, the Expectation that I am to make a Genius of him whom his Maker has made a dunce. . . .

There is no clearer evidence of Maturin's commitment to literature than the fact that during these extremely trying years Maturin wrote *The Milesian Chief,* the best of his first three novels.

In *The Milesian Chief,* Maturin realizes where his real powers are to be found—in "darkening the gloomy, and of deepening the sad; of painting life in extremes,"; and in the characters and plot he chose for his third novel, he created the circumstances to evoke these talents. He has come to realize the potential of Ireland itself as a setting in which to explore his favorite themes and recognizes that Italy is not the only country where romance, violence, and the incredible exist side by side. As he says in his preface, ". . . I have chosen my own country for the scene, because I believe it the only country on earth, where, from the strange existing opposition of religion, politics, and manners, the extremes of refinement and barbarism are united, and the most wild and incredible situations of romantic story are hourly passing before modern eyes."

But not only does *The Milesian Chief* represent Maturin's attempt to synthesize the strongest aspects of his first two novels; it also represents a further advancement of his style and technique in exploring what he calls "the obscure recesses of the human heart." In his first novel, Maturin used the conventions of a genre which, as he was later to admit, had already passed its zenith. Although he returns to the gothic techniques again in works such as *Bertram* and, of course, *Melmoth,* he does so only after exploring in *The Milesian Chief* the possibilities of touching those realms of our psychic life most affected by the gothic genre without actually employing the machinery of the gothic. He still employs some of the devices of the gothic, but he consciously downplays such devices. "In my first work," Maturin wrote, "I attempted to explore the ground forbidden to man, the sources of visionary terror; the 'formless and the void:' in my present I have tried the equally obscure recesses of the human heart." Since the world of gothic fiction, its castles, dungeons, spirits, and cruelties, is often simply a macrocosm of the inhabitants who people it, such a transition was a natural one for Maturin. In *Montorio* he had explored the fears, anxieties, and desires of man as he projects them outside of him; he now turns to the source of the projections itself, a region "equally obscure," if not more so.

The Milesian Chief storyline is intricate, focusing on the fate of two brothers, Connal and Desmond O'Morven, the former a leader of the Irish rebels and the latter an officer in the British regiment, trying to track down the rebels. They are the sons of Randall O'Morven, a son of an old Milesian Chief. Randall had married the sister of Lord Montclare, the present owner of the ruined family's estates, and is presently the land-steward of Lord Montclare's land. The novel consists of the independent stories of the two brothers, but is constructed in such a way that the two stories intersect frequently, culminating in the death of the two brothers before the same firing squad. As in *Montorio*, the owner of the estates is always accompanied by a priest, Father Morosini, who holds over him the secret that Lord

Montclare had, with the priest's help, incarcerated his wife and spread the rumor of her death because she had failed to produce a male heir. Only later in the novel do we find out that the wife actually had a child, a girl, and that she, with Morosini's help, had convinced Montclare that it was a son. But Montclare cannot acknowledge this child without also admitting his treatment of his wife and thus is, when the novel opens, fleeing from country to country with another daughter, Armida.

Armida is a graceful and accomplished but rather superficial young girl. Falling in love with Connal, who several times saves her life after she and her father arrive in Ireland, she commits herself wholly to him, even following him to his rebel camp hidden in the mountains. She is, however, forced to marry Desmond, Connal's brother, by Lady Montclare, who has returned to Ireland with her "son," Endymion (who is actually Ines, her daughter who has—and here Maturin casts all probability to the wind—been kept ignorant of her sex.) But Armida takes poison and dies at the same moment that Desmond and Connal are shot. Endymion and Desmond's love affair makes up the other main storyline in the novel, and in it Maturin again skirts, this time much more explicitly, the theme of homosexual love. But as in the case of Cyprian and Ippolito in *Montorio,* Endymion is in fact a girl and thus their love is homosexual in appearance only. Ines, like Armida, virtually goes insane as a result of the agonies she endures at the hands of Lady Montclare, and she too dies at the novel's conclusion. Thus the last few pages of the *Milesian Chief,* with the almost simultaneous death of four major characters, have a mortality rate reminiscent of Webster or Tourneur. Only the chief perpetrator of evil, Lady Montclare, escapes death; but in sending her to a convent for the rest of her life, Maturin probably felt that he was assigning her a fate worse than death.

If *The Milesian Chief* shares some aspects of plot and character in common with Maturin's first two novels, it is quite different in the use he makes of these similarities. First of all, it is much more successful in its discussion of Ireland and its people. Whereas in *The Wild Irish Boy* one has the feeling that the setting was for the most part tacked on to the plot line, in this novel both the historical and the geographical setting contribute to the novel's theme. Here Maturin allows himself the time and the setting to speak of the country his "heart is full of":"grey and showery sky; . . . her gloom . . . her misty heath, her bleak shore, the sullen song of her storms, . . . her caves, and her oceans. . . . " But the chords that Ireland struck in Maturin's heart also contained some dissonant tones, for Maturin observes that "the country is bleeding under ignorance, poverty, and superstition, and we cast over its wounds a gay embroidered garment of voluptuousness, beneath which the heavings and shudderings of its agony are but more frightfully visible." Maturin is one of the first writers to explore the nature of the contradiction between the stereotype Irishman—wild, hard-drinking, fun-loving—and the sorrow and poverty concealed by it.

Placing the action of the novel after the Rebellion of 1798, Maturin has the opportunity to deal directly with the political and social tensions of the time. In setting brother against brother, he tries to find a symbol to convey the nature of the conflicts created by civil war, and although Desmond and Connal never engage in direct combat, the dissension within the families that frequently exists in civil war is artistically realized by Maturin. Connal is the novel's most romantic figure and his exploits and his endurance sometimes go beyond credibility, yet Maturin clearly shows him to be as much a victim of time and circumstance as the rest of the novel's characters. He is in love with Ireland—its mythology, its music, and its history—but is always aware of the distinction between Ireland's past greatness and the reality of the present political and economic situation.

Maturin creates in the two brothers potential figures of romance, but at the same time suggests the danger of allowing romantic illusion to gain control of one's vision. War in the abstract is heroic and noble; but in the concrete, it results in death, mutilation, and agony. Connal does not see war as heroic and ennobling, and he makes it clear that time and circumstance rather than personal inclination have made him a rebel. Maturin develops this conflict within Connal in a decisive manner and shows considerable improvement in character development since *The Wild Irish Boy*. In Connal we also see the elaboration of one of Maturin's favorite themes—the danger of abstracting or idealizing virtues to such an extent that we use them to rationalize or conceal evil deeds and motives. One of the most fascinating aspects of Connal is his recognition of the disparity between words and the deeds we commit in their names and his simultaneous awareness that he must act, in spite of this recognition.

If patriotism and religion are often employed by the

human mind to justify agony and pain on a grand scale, it is love that most often causes pain on the personal level. Maturin's treatment of love is one of his most interesting—and most enigmatic—aspects, primarily because one is never quite sure of his perspective toward his material. Sometimes he is clearly outside of and critical toward the relationships he depicts; at other times, he seems to participate in the very attitudes of which he has elsewhere shown the dangers. The character of Armida is perhaps the most clearly realized and developed in the novel. Quite early, it is observed that "her talents are real, but her character is artificial." The rest of the novel is devoted to creating in her a woman who slowly and painfully realizes her true character through her love for Connal. She is one of Maturin's most beautifully drawn women and her courage, her resentments, her vacillations, and her gradual recognition of self come forth vividly.

However, other themes are responsible for the perplexity one feels when trying to discover a consistent pattern in Maturin's attitudes toward love. In so far as he shows both the destructive and the ennobling qualities of love, Maturin is within a tradition running from Plato to Shakespeare. But in order to understand why he so often views love as a force leading to death or insanity, we have to consider his strong Calvinistic leanings. He says in one of his letters to Scott that "I am a high Calvinist in my Religious opinions" and, his love of the good life and his scathing critique of the Calvinistic temperament in *Women* notwithstanding, he maintains throughout his writings a strong Calvinistic outlook. The world for him is an abode that constantly tempts and threatens its inhabitants. Madness, sickness, and death seem to be its predominant characteristics, and happiness is most often a fleeting and transient gossamer that few succeed in capturing. Analogous to this world view is his vision of man aspiring to the spiritual and transcendent, whether through love or religion, yet forever victimized by a body filled with errant emotions and passions.

It is in Maturin's women that we most often see this tension between the physical and spiritual. Armida, for example, is described in a "visionary light . . . her faint ethereal garb . . . strongly contrasted by the vivid crimson of her cheek." Elsewhere in the novel, we hear her described as "voluptuous and timid," as a siren enticing men to their destruction, and as a "devil." In the novel's minor female characters, the spiritual often totally succumbs to the sensual through the device of love: one young girl falls in love with Connal and later tells Armida that "from that minute I gave myself up to a wicked mind; I was a likely girl, and I thought I might please him as well as another." She rapidly moves from the love for one man to a desire for many, later becoming Desmond's mistress.

In the opposition between the "visionary light" and that "crimson of her cheek," and in the plight of the lesser female characters, we see the tension between the spiritual and the physical and also man's precarious relationship to his own body. Maturin frequently writes of the dangers of trying to sublimate or repress one's sexuality and of how fanaticism, cruelty, and loss of human feelings can result from such attempts; but at the same time, there is in his writings a strong fear of the body and disgust of sensuality. The love that humans, as opposed to angels, experience must necessarily involve the physical as well as the spiritual and this alone is enough to make love in Maturin's fiction inherently destructive. Men and women are doomed not by their faults and weaknesses so much as by the unavoidable fact that they are human. It is in this respect that Maturin seems closest to his contemporary, Lord Byron. In both, we see the affirmation of love's redemptive powers coupled with a sense that by falling in love one repeats man's original fall from paradise; in both we see an attraction and a repulsion by the human body. In Maturin the sensualist is barely held in check by the Calvinist, but the check is always there.

When we recognize this often paradoxical attitude of Maturin's toward love, we can better understand why the theme of homosexual love recurs in his writings. The strongest example of this is in *The Milesian Chief* in the love relationship between Desmond and Endymion (or Ines). Maturin is describing a love affair between two persons, each of whom believes the other to be of the same sex as himself. In *The Milesian Chief*, the treatment is much stronger and much more explicit:

> O torture me no more with this fantastic fondness . . . so unlike what we ought to feel for each other. . . . Never did I feel before these wild, these maddening sensations. I know not what you have done with me; what strange influence you have obtained over me, but it is an influence that I must fly from to preserve my reason, my life. . . . Oh, untwine those arms from me; you are making me wild; by blood burns like fire in my veins . . . they are tears of hatred—hatred of myself and you.

Maturin's recurrent treatment of homosexual love can only partially be explained by his fascination with the unknown and taboo realms of human experience; he also uses homosexual love to explore the nature of heterosexual love. It is for him at once a more etheralized and transcendent love and also a love more filled with passion, guilt, and danger. In this respect, homosexual love is a surrogate for heterosexual love in the extreme. Maturin's fear of the body and of sexuality is, as it were, legitimized by locating the fear within a taboo topic. The homosexual love he depicts is a love that is always potential and never fulfilled, one more fraught with peril than the love between man and woman, but also one in which both internal and external pressures provide a check to prevent a complete commitment. In one place, Desmond can refer to his love for Endymion as "a love passing that of women" while simultaneously being racked by the guilt he feels for such a love. This is very much the case of Maturin's own attitude toward love in his art: he speaks of it as ennobling and rewarding but shows it to be an emotion generating the forces of its own destruction and the destruction of those who yield to it.

The Milesian Chief was the first of Maturin's novels for which he actually received some financial reward, being paid eighty pounds by Colburn the publisher for the copyright. This payment was paltry when compared to the financial success Maturin was to realize from *Bertram* four years later, but it was roughly equivalent to one year's salary for a curate, and it must have been extremely satisfying to him under the circumstances. At the end of the preface to *The Milesian Chief*, Maturin indicates that he has committed himself to writing and that regardless of the success his first three novels enjoyed, he "shall write again." He did write again, although not until four years later, but in the meantime he began a correspondence with Sir Walter Scott that was to continue until Maturin's death.

Scott, in a review of a number of Gothic novels, had singled out Maturin's *Montorio* as showing evidence of "a remarkable instance of genius degraded by the labour in which it is employed," and advised the young author "to seek one on whose taste and judgment he can rely," concluding that "there is much in these volumes which promises a career that may at some future time astonish the public." Scott's review was published in 1810, but it was not until December of 1812 that Maturin, having learned the identity of the reviewer, wrote his first letter to Scott. It is the sort of letter one might expect a young and unrecognized author would write to a man of Scott's fame—reticent and yet clearly seeking Scott's "taste and judgment." In the next couple of letters they exchanged Scott gives Maturin some advice—"literature though an excellent staff has always proved a wretched crutch to those who relied upon it entirely for support"—and Maturin in turn reveals to Scott much of his history and his present circumstances. It is evident from his letters that Maturin not only needed a counselor who might be able to assert influence in the right places, but also someone to whom he could unburden his fears and his hopes.

Once having been turned to for his "taste and judgment," Scott proved to be an excellent literary adviser to Maturin. In his comments about *Bertram*, which

Maturin submitted for criticism and suggestions, Scott is encouraging and yet frank about its faults:

> In general I like it very much indeed, and so does a friend of superior taste to whom I read it—The Character of Bertram is highly dramatic, well-got up and maintained with a Satanic dignity which is often truly sublime—the Lady Imogine may be also considered as a master-piece, and the language throughout is beautiful even to redundance. . . .

Its defects, he goes on to say, include a redundance of language, the figure of the Black Knight, and the slowness with which the last two acts bring the play to a close. Concluding with words that must have been quite gratifying to Maturin, Scott writes "in fact you are in the happy predicament of needing only the pruning knife. I will be much honoured by standing Godfather to Bertram and accept the compliment willingly."

2

The Middle Years, 1816–1819

Scott's praise of *Bertram* and his hopes for its eventual success were probably small comfort to Maturin, whose situation was at this time desperate and whose mood was verging on despair. In 1813, Maturin had generously but foolishly provided the security necessary for a relative to borrow a large sum of money. The relative soon became bankrupt and the whole debt was transferred to Maturin. Burdened with this additional drain on his income, Maturin was facing ruin by the last months of 1814:

> the only real evil of life is coming fast upon me—horrid actual want is staring me in the Face—unable to get academical pupils, unsuccessful *even in my attempt to open a day-school,* unsought, unemployed, the utmost exertion of human economy unable to bring my Expenditure for *bare necessaries* within the bounds of my wretched income, debts increasing, means decreasing, such is my present prospect.

His overriding concern, as one might expect, was to get as much money as possible from his writings. He thought of bringing *Bertram* out in London solely in "the hope of the profit being greater, the only object of any consequence to me in the disposal of my literary attempts."

After the London prospect was discouraged by a letter from John Kemble, Maturin entertained some hopes of having it produced in Dublin, but "afterwards reflected that it might be injurious to my character, as a Clergyman and still more as a teacher, one of my pupils having been removed on the bare report of my having written a play." It was more than a year after Maturin had originally submitted the manuscript of *Bertram* to Scott before the prospects for its production began to brighten. Maturin, on Scott's advise, had sent the manuscript to Lord Byron, who had in 1815 been appointed to a Committee of Management of the Drury Lane Theatre. Byron, like Scott, was enthusiastic about it and in December of 1815 wrote to Maturin commending its "great and singular merit." Besides lending Maturin fifty pounds, Byron gave Maturin some valuable advice, namely that Maturin allow George Lamb, a co-member of Byron's Committee, to adapt the drama for the stage. During the early months of 1816, Lamb corresponded frequently with Maturin, submitting detailed, lengthy, and intelligent suggestions about *Bertram:*

> In the first place the strain of vehement passion is too unvaried throughout the play, not merely for the feelings of the Audience, but for the powers of any Actor to support. The Characters of Bertram and Imogine are of such length, so constantly on the Stage, and never except in situations of agitation and passion; that there are no performers whose physical strength would not sink under them before half the play was over. There is also too great a succession of long speeches . . . The Dark Knight of the Forest and all relating to him should clearly be cut out: He is a personage who would be unintelligible to the majority of the audience, or if intelligible, offensive.

Lamb's advice was taken, though at times reluctantly, and on May 9, 1816, *Bertram: of The Castle of St. Aldobrand* was performed at Drury Lane Theatre, with Edmund Kean, the famous British actor, starring in the lead role of Bertram.

Its success overwhelmed even its most ardent supporters. Maturin received £350 for the copyright and was finally to realize nearly £1000 from *Bertram*, by far his most financially successful work. In reading the play, it is difficult to account for its spectacular success. Its popularity as a play might in part be attributed to the acting abilities of Kean and to a drought of talent in the British theatre at the time; but the published edition—rushed to press without altering a line from the stage version—went through seven printings in its first year. *Bertram* undoubtedly benefitted from the great popularity of Byron's *Childe Harold's Pilgrimage*, the first two cantos of which had been published in 1812, for the hero of Maturin's play was spoken of by a number of contemporary critics as a "Byronic figure." Maturin himself, however, was to maintain that he could never read more than the beginning of Byron's major works, and the figure of Bertram is clearly anticipated in Maturin's own earlier writings. Isolated from society and driven by remorse and anger into deeds of violence, Bertram is a descendant of Father Schemoli and Connal O'Morven. Bertram had once enjoyed considerable power as the favorite of the court, but his increased prestige aroused the fears of those in power, notably Lord Aldobrand, whose scheming finally led to Bertram's being forced to flee into exile. Upon his flight, Bertram gathered a band of robbers, and as the play opens, their ship is capsizing off the coast near Lord Aldobrand's castle. As fate would have it, the unconscious Bertram, having been saved from drowning, is taken to Lord Aldobrand's castle for shelter.

There he discovers that Imogine, the girl he had loved, had married Lord Aldobrand in order to save her aged father from starving. Bertram conceives of the plan of revenging himself upon Aldobrand by seducing Imogine while Aldobrand is away. He succeeds in carrying out his plans, but upon hearing that Aldobrand is returning with his army to capture him, Bertram, no longer satisfied with his original plan, ambushes and slays Aldobrand. Imogine, who had stood by silently while her husband was killed, is driven insane by guilt and remorse and escapes to a secluded cave. Bertram is captured at the scene of his crime, and as he is being led to execution by his captors, he passes the cave and sees the demented figure of Imogine. She confronts him with the enormity of his crime and then she dies, upon which Bertram, also stricken with guilt, steals a knife from a guard and slays himself.

Between Maturin's original conception of Bertram and the final figure as he appeared on stage, much is lost and consequently the passion and grandeur with which the hero was originally invested are not dramatically realized. The plot of the published play is melodramatic and inadequate to support the hero as he is described in the drama. Very little of Bertram's "evil-strength, so above earthly pitch" is seen and consequently we have difficulty believing the Prior when he refers to Bertram as a "High-hearted man, sublime even in thy guilt,/Whose passions are thy crime, whose angel-sin/Is pride that rivals the star-bright apostate's." Maturin had intended for Bertram to be a man driven by his own internal passions and also by demonic forces with which he conspires: Bertram, speaking of his hatred for Aldobrand, says that "I would consort with mine eternal enemy,/To be revenged on him." The play clearly demands fulfillment of Bertram's vow to join forces with whatever powers are necessary, but once the character of the Dark Knight was taken out of the play, such a fulfillment was impossible.

Scott had been the first to recommend dropping the figure of the Black Knight, but his later letters suggest that he was never able to rest easily with this advice. In his 1818 review of *Women: or Pour et Contre,* Scott included the scenes that had been deleted, and these make one regret the final exclusion of this strange figure. Without the Black Knight, Bertram's Heathcliff-like qualities are unaccounted for and he often seems little more than an ill-tempered and treacherous bandit. As Scott came to see, our emotional response to Bertram depends upon our recognition that he is both victim and victimizer. Scott's original advice to eliminate the Black Knight was supported by Byron and Lamb, and Maturin reluctantly followed it; but even the play's success did not reconcile him to its emasculation. Complaining that "they have printed it as acted," he argued "whatever tends to Efface the radical distinctions of intellectual character, and reduce all the wild and wayward shoots of Mind, stubbed, unsightly and grotesque as they may be, to one smooth-shave Level, by the ponderous operation of the Critical Roller—whoever does this, does mischief. . . . I have no power of affecting, no hope of instructing, no play or other production of mine will ever draw a tear from the eye, or teach a lesson to the Heart, so I wish they would let me do what I am good for, sit down by my magic Cauldron, mix my dark ingredients, see the bubbles work, and the spirits rise, and by the pale and mystic light, I might show them 'the best of my delights'."

The distance between Maturin and the Church was further widened by *Bertram's* popularity. In order to protect his authorship, Maturin had to drop the pseudonym used for his first three novels and finally to identify himself in print as The Reverend C. R. Maturin. Rumors immediately began to circulate that he was to be deprived of his curacy in consequence of having written *Bertram*, but nothing came of the rumor, and Maturin remained in his position until his death.

On the other hand, Maturin and his collaborators on the stage production of *Bertram* felt sure that he was at last assured of fame and the managers of Drury Lane Theatre begged him to follow his success as soon as possible with another drama. Heartened by praise and hoping to attain independence from the Church through another such success, Maturin began working on his next drama almost immediately. In September of 1816, he described the drama he was working on as centered around a character who "bears a joint resemblance to Lear and Titus Andronicus (in *passion* not in *situation*) . . ." He created the lead role with the actor, Edmund Kean, specifically in mind, and his hopes during the composition of *Manuel* were high.

Manuel opened at Drury Lane on March 8, 1817 and ran for only five nights. Maturin's friends put the blame on Kean, who had lost all interest in playing "a character of hoary and decrepid distress" and consequently played the role very badly. Maturin himself limited his observations to the fact that "it has not pleased," but was later to admit that it was a bad play. He had again hoped to capitalize upon an understanding of the public's tastes and this attempt also had backfired. The play concerns the story of Manuel, an old and rich Spanish nobleman, and his great love for his son Alonzo, a hero in Spain's wars against the Moors. Blinded by his love for his son, Manuel has neglected DeZelos, a relative whom he has allowed to live in great poverty. DeZelos, seething with resentment, conspires to have Alonzo assassinated. Most of the play centers around the conflict between Manuel, who is certain of DeZelos' complicity in Alonzo's disappearance, and DeZelos' attempts to have Manuel exiled so that he can gain his riches. DeZelos succeeds in having Manuel and his daughter, Victoria, exiled for spreading slanders, but eventually one of the assassins, stricken by guilt for Alonzo's death, reveals, in the presence of Manuel, DeZelos, and their children, the knife of the man responsible for Alonzo's death. DeZelos' name appears on the blade, and he, seeing his plans in ruins, grabs the knife and kills himself. Manuel sees his revenge completed and also dies. Critics immediately attacked the absurd improbability that a man would hire an assassin and then give him a knife engraved with his own name with which to commit the crime. The ending, however, is by no means the play's only weakness.

Bertram had been criticized for drawing no tears, and in *Manuel*, by choosing as his subject "a maiden's constancy and a father's woe," Maturin seems to be trying to compensate for the lack of pathos in his first drama. But Manuel is no King Lear and his daughter is definitely no Cordelia. In the characterization of DeZelos, however, Maturin handles the problem of motivation with considerable skill, and in his sections depicting hatred, contempt, and jealousy, Maturin displays a bitingly caustic wit seen only sporadically in his fiction. *Bertram* was almost devoid of tenderness or pity, but during the closing scenes between Manuel and Victoria, Maturin is clearly experimenting with the delineation of those emotions and preparing himself for those beautiful and moving scenes between Melmoth and Immalee that he was later to create. But *Manuel* is a mixture of too many dramatic modes to be a dramatic success itself. It aspires to create its hero after the tragic mode, but totally lacks the vision we find in tragedy; it has the characteristics of Restoration comedy in the fawning, flattery, and obsequiousness of its minor characters, but without the double entendres, the wit, and the particular morality of the Restoration stage; and, finally, it has the plot line of a later nineteenth-century melodrama, but lacks that self-consciousness of form that makes the Victorian melodrama so delightful. (Though some of the weaknesses of *Manuel* may be due to the revisions it underwent at the hands of the theater committee, such unpublished scenes as did appear in print later are not strong enough to have compensated for *Manuel's* weaknesses.)

Although Maturin had made a good deal of money from *Bertram,* he was not much better off in 1818 than he had been in 1815. Most of the money he had received went to pay off his relative's debt and the rest had been spent recklessly. The spectacular fame of *Bertram* had made Maturin giddy, and, certain of continuing success, he had lived far beyond his means. Consequently *Manuel's* failure was doubly upsetting to him, but it did finally convince him of the folly of trying to anticipate something so elusive as "public taste," and in the future he relied on his own taste and judgement.

Women: or Pour et Contre was published in Edinburgh in 1818. In its own way, it is as much of a masterpiece as *Melmoth* and is equally representative of Maturin's fascination with the "obscure recesses of the human heart," and of the skill with which he guides us through these recesses. In *Women*, Maturin finds for the first time a perfect combination for all of his talents as a novelist and creates a work which, though preeminently a psychological novel within a realistic framework, contains elements of the historical novel, the romance, and the gothic. And in his portrayal of the two heroines, Eva and Zaira, Maturin is so skillful that a number of years would pass before novelists would treat with comparable sensitivity and insight the themes he pursues. Maturin had said of *Women* that "it will set the evangelical world in arms, if they read it." It is a biting and perceptive analysis of Evangelicalism—of the increasing power and wealth of the Evangelicals, of the ways in which they used the Sabbath School system to proselytize their beliefs and of the various societies they established. Particularly in the figure of Mr. Wentworth, Maturin captures that mixture of worldliness and piety, of capitalistic initiative and Calvinistic ardor, of secular goals "justified" by divine providence.

But although it contains an indictment of Evangelicalism and the hypocrisy it engendered, *Women* is primarily Maturin's further exploration of the psychological and physical nature of love as experienced by its three central characters, Charles De Courcy, Eva Wentworth, and Zaira Dalmatiani, and as such, it is one of Maturin's masterpieces. Compared to his earlier novels, the plot line is slim and the conflicts are internalized. The story revolves around the love that De Courcy experiences for Eva and for Zaira, and, in turn, the love of the two women for him. De Courcy's love in both cases is accompanied by frustration—with Eva because of her strong Calvinistic background and her consequent fear of human passions, and with Zaira because she wishes to maintain an intellectual, nonphysical relationship with him. Driven to Zaira because of Eva's inability or unwillingness to reciprocate his love, Charles falls in love with Zaira and travels to France with her while still engaged to Eva. Tiring of Zaira, he eventually returns to Eva after a brief liaison with another woman, but Eva is dying and refuses to see him. At the novel's end, Zaira discovers that the young woman from whom she stole Charles is in reality her own daughter. Eva's death makes any reconciliation between Zaira and Charles impossible and Charles, weakened by disease and exhaustion, soon dies at the age of nineteen.

In view of such a conclusion, it is obvious that Maturin is not writing a conventional love story. Maturin chooses a setting that contains, as he states in his preface, "a paucity of characters and incidents," and thereby gives himself freedom to explore more fully the various aspects of love. When we first meet Eva, she is young, innocent, and deeply committed to the faith of her family. In Maturin's description of her "ethereal lightness and purity, a visible sanctity," we see shades of Byron's Haidee and Maturin's own Immalee. Contrasted to her is Zaira, sensuous, dark-haired, older, and already experienced in life, having been seduced and married at the age of fifteen. But they are each vulnerable to love's destructive passions.

In this novel, as in *The Milesian Chief*, Maturin's depiction of love is complex and double-edged. On the one hand, he is critical of the unnaturalness of denying one's physicality and aware of the painful consequences of trying to sublimate all traces of human love into religious devotion. For all of her innocence, Eva is as much the destroyer as the destroyed. In one place, Charles, rebuffed by Eva, stops visiting her, "for he felt he could no longer support the sight of the face whose every glance seemed to be drinking up his blood." The image of Eva as vampire is quite appropriate, for in her unearthliness she demands of Charles more than is humanly possible to give, and in escaping from her, he simply affirms through action that he must recognize his physical as well as spiritual needs. Similarly, Maturin shows how Eva's sexuality, though consciously denied, is nevertheless sublimely present in a religion charged with passionate and erotic undertones.

Maturin realized that sexual asceticism is not limited to women alone, for Charles is entrapped as much by his idealization of woman as by his passions. Attracted to Eva and experiencing strange and unaccountable emotions for the first time, Charles views these new emotions as sacrilege against Eva as well as against the pure concept of love he had previously held. For both of them, the guilt that arises from the violation of previously held ideals manifests itself in suffering: in Eva's case, in a self-imposed isolation during which she tries, through penance and suffering, to rarify her love for Charles into a love exclusively for Christ; and for Charles, in a physical sickness and deterioration brought about by the strong and irreconcilable conflicts within him. Again, we see a conflict in Maturin as well. For the most part, he is clearly critical of the sexual repression, but at the same time he seems implicitly to share some of the attitudes of his characters, or at least he creates a world view that supports their validity. In one respect, the story of the love between Eva and Charles (and between Zaira and Charles) is the story of a love that could perhaps have been happily resolved had they been able to free themselves from those demands that seem to invariably destroy any chance for a satisfactory relationship. But in another respect, it is not so much personal inadequacies that bring about sorrow and suffering as it is the nature of love itself. Love carries the seed of its own destruction, and when man falls in love, the force is released that will inevitably cause pain. Man is born into a fallen world and, since only innocence can assure felicity, the fact that innocence must be lost guarantees the omnipresence of suffering. Maturin speaks directly of this harsh reality: "That 'man was made to mourn' is not merely the sentiment of a poet . . . it is the experience, the daily terrible experience of life." Few of Maturin's marriages are happy, and those which simply manage to avoid unhappiness are exceptional enough to evoke surprise.

Women, however, is Maturin's fullest attempt to work within a realistic framework and to account for the actions of the characters not in terms of a larger system imposed upon them, but in terms of their own weakness and strengths. The motivations and behavior of the three central characters are depicted with a strength and a self-confidence that Maturin only possesses when he is writing according to his own artistic desires. The latter part of the novel has been criticized for being too long and insufficiently integrated with the rest, but Maturin's analysis of Zaira's anguish contains some of his most astute psychological insights. Prefiguring some later nineteenth-century female characters, such as Flaubert's Emma Bovary and Hardy's Sue Bridehead, Zaira interprets the pain she suffers as arising from a personal transgression and consequently turns to religion in hopes of doing penance and alleviating her inner sense of guilt. This analysis of Zaira's religious anguish, of the spiritual and sensuous vying for power within her, stands almost by itself among nineteenth-century British novels, since the depiction of religious experiences was traditionally left to poetry, confession and tract.

In writing of Eva, most critics have concurred with Scott's description of her—"so soft, so gentle, so self-devoted—such a mixture of the purity of heaven with the simplicity of earth." Maturin does depict her as a young woman too ethereal to sustain for long those shocks and vicissitudes that this world and her own emotions visit upon her. It is likely that he modeled Eva upon a niece of his, Susan Lea, who, after a long sickness, died at the age of 18. Yet Eva is a fictional character and, moreover, one toward whom Maturin is by no means wholly sympathetic. In Eva, we see a young woman whose capacity to experience life has been tragically stunted by a narrow religion that she not only inherits but manages to sustain through sheer assertion of will.

Eva is certainly neither so coarse nor so dogmatic as those Evangelicals who surround her; but the deficiencies from which she suffers, though drawn with more gentleness and sympathy, are those which Maturin attributes to Evangelicalism in particular and to religious fanaticism in general. She is described as one for whom "religion seemed to be an instinct, a part of her pure nature," but Maturin, in calling attention to her "expressions that indicated sighs suppressed," indicates that her religion is not natural, but depends rather upon suppression of those instincts that might have given her the will to live. Charles De Courcy realizes that her love for him is but an extension of her death-oriented existence and that her idea of mutual love is the simultaneous dissolving of two bodies into pure spirit. Maturin's final attitude toward her is ambivalent. He is attracted to her sincerity and beauty but repulsed by her harsh and unforgiving Evangelicalism. At the end of the novel, we see this ambivalence in the manner with which he depicts Eva's death. On one hand, she possesses a faith and wisdom that almost certainly correspond to Maturin's own beliefs, and yet her death-bed scene reads like a parody of Evangelical tracts of the late 18th and early 19th centuries. She emphasizes the necessity of keeping our eye on death, the futility and destructiveness of worldly vanities, and the harshness of the task of life that God imposes upon us. In her final absurd pronouncement of love for Charles—"What more could I do than die for him,"—Maturin is showing the cost a human being pays when he tries to deny or suppress his humanity. Zaira, during her sufferings over her love for Charles, had also attempted to gain absolution through a monastic life, but she rejects it because she sees it as "torpid, obtuse, self-contracted, self-sufficed, without malevolence or kindness, pleasure or pain, love or grief."

The money Maturin received for *Women* again relieved his immediate financial worries. He was, however, still upset over the failure of *Manuel* and had started working on a new tragedy as early as April, 1817. Convinced of Kean's responsibility for *Manuel's* failure, Maturin was determined not to create his next tragedy around any one actor. Most of *Fredolfo* was probably written during 1818, and, on the advice of George Lamb, Maturin submitted the play to Covent Garden rather than to Drury Lane. Lamb again acted as Maturin's literary adviser, suggesting that he "take care the first act is not too good, which was the principal fault of *Manuel.*" In spite of this timely and enigmatic advice, *Fredolfo* opened at Covent Garden in the spring of 1819 and failed even more badly than *Manuel*.

It is a matter of speculation why a particular play fails; but in *Fredolfo's* case, the reasons advanced were the absence of one leading role, the disinterestedness of the major actors, the ineptitude of the minor ones, and the violence and treachery of its characters, especially during the closing acts. Another reason, however, was probably the fact that *Fredolfo* was too strong for its audience to take. It is hard to imagine what Coleridge, who reacted so vehemently to the presence of adultery in *Bertram*, might have said about *Fredolfo*. It is not great drama—the stage was not the proper medium for Maturin's particular talents—but on the other hand, it is a much better play than the eminently successful *Bertram*.

Fredolfo, set in 14th century Switzerland, revolves around the character Fredolfo who had, many years before, killed a man who had raped his wife. This man was Wallenberg, the Austrian governor; his son, the present governor, is still seeking his father's killer. The murder had been witnessed by a Swiss peasant named Adelmar. Exiled to keep the secret, Adelmar has since returned to Switzerland and has been thrown into a dungeon by Fredolfo. Urilda, Fredolfo's daughter, had fallen in love with Adelmar after he saved her life, and has persuaded her father to spare his life. Berthold, whose love for Urilda has been rejected, reveals in anger to Wallenberg that Fredolfo is the murderer of his father, and Fredolfo and Urilda are then imprisoned. Adelmar is also captured but succeeds in engineering the escape of all three prisoners. Wallenberg finally captures Urilda again in a church and, using her as a hostage, forces Fredolfo and Adelmar to lay down their weapons. He kills the defenseless Adelmar, but is himself killed by the enraged Fredolfo; and as the play closes, Urilda dies next to Adelmar, scorning her father's attempts to console her.

The play obviously contains much violence, but none of the violence is gratuitous. The English audience did not object so much to the subject of rape raised by the play as they did to Wallenberg's final cowardly act of disarming Adelmar and then killing him. But this action is perfectly in keeping with Wallenberg's sadistic and tyrannical character. Maturin does a superb job of introducing quickly and dramatically the major characters and setting the mood of tension. But what makes this drama superior to his first two plays is the skill with which he probes into the nature of guilt, violence, and evil. It is the aspect of *Fredolfo* that most clearly prefigures *Melmoth* and, like that work, *Fredolfo* has to be understood primarily in psychological terms.

In a letter to Alaric Watts, Maturin writes:

> I must revert to the part of Berthold, which is sufficiently eccentric and extravagant. Don't let him, on my account, appear a ludicrous figure. . . . don't let him be ludicrous, that must be the ruin of the play. No one could bear a *Kitchen Richard.* Much depends on Berthold.

When he observes that "much depends on Berthold," Maturin is absolutely correct. He is the play's pivotal character, not only illuminating our understanding of the other major characters, especially Fredolfo and Wallenberg, but also himself moving toward a symbolic role as the embodiment of evil and the demonic. However, Berthold is also a man and his human dimensions are dramatically conveyed by Maturin, for we see both his anguish and his frustrated tenderness. Far from being a ludicrous figure, he asks for our sympathy because of his suffering and arouses our fear because of the violence that this suffering can provoke. Incapable of creating or sharing pleasure, he uses his power to convert the world around him into an arena of pain in which the anguish of others serves to diminish his own isolation.

It is in his capacity as inflictor of pain and punishment that Berthold approaches a symbolic role. For, in spite of his weakness and deformity, Berthold exerts a control over Fredolfo from which he cannot escape; in fact, Berthold is the play's moral agent, and it is in relation to him that we judge the actions of the other characters. He is not, of course, a moral agent in terms of the good that he might perpetrate, but in the evil he evokes from others. In one place, Fredolfo speaks of himself as a man who is "enthralled to one, who wreaks on me a daemon's mockery, and a daemon's malice." In *Bertram* Maturin had wanted to explore the demonic through the Dark Knight; in *Fredolfo*, by using the figure of a grotesque and misshapen human, Maturin is able to do so, and, at the same time, succeed in keeping his play intact. As the play advances, the relationship of Fredolfo and Berthold is powerfully delineated, and Berthold, in his ugliness and great capacity for violence, comes to symbolize the subrational and the nonpublic part of Fredolfo, "his country's hero and champion." Berthold is a constant reminder of Fredolfo's past and present guilt; as Fredolfo describes him, "Berthold lives in vivid consciousness,/The wakeful demon of the buried secret."

The presence of this "wakeful demon" in every man fascinated Maturin. Again and again, he explores its presence and the ways in which it makes itself manifest, no matter how deeply buried or how strenuously repressed. When Fredolfo screams in rage against Berthold, he is raging against that part of himself that belies the nobility and heroism of his public self:

> Thou nightmare of the oppressed sight, on whom
> Deformity ran wanton! Yes, she scratched
> The page where Nature would have written man,
> And madly scrawl'd it with a pictured devil!

It is in the other major character, that of the younger Wallenberg, that Maturin suggests that the antithesis between man and devil is not so clear as Fredolfo's statement implies. If Berthold represents the demonic counterpart of Fredolfo, he also represents the human counterpart of Wallenberg. When we first meet them, the two men seem very dissimilar. One is a weak, deformed, and impotent servant and the other is a powerful and vicious governor, but they share the desire for Fredolfo's downfall. In Wallenberg's character, Maturin probes the sources of rage and evil and, in doing so, suggests that Wallenberg is but a Berthold without the physical deformity. However, his character is not so fully developed as Berthold's in that there does not seem to be adequate motivation for his rage and fury. In Berthold's case, our compassion is stirred by a man who, despite his twisted body and deranged mind, does possess traces of gentleness and love and who could have been capable of tenderness. Wallenberg gives no indication of tender feelings, and even when he speaks of his feelings for Urilda, "Round whom I could, like the dark serpent, fold,/ To twine, and—ha! to crush thee," the language of love is only a vehicle for his violence and sadism. Critics who have questioned what seems to be the excessive and capricious capacity of Wallenberg for violence have overlooked the fact that in his characterization of Wallenberg, Maturin in not interested in conventional causality, but in a psychological study of evil.

In *Fredolfo*, Maturin further develops the theme of repression giving rise to cruelty, and depicts the sexual quality of sadism, torture, and murder. Wallenberg envisions torturing Fredolfo in front of his daughter, and in his heavily eroticized fantasies, we see evidence of a nature that can realize sexual excitement only vicariously and only through pain and suffering. Wallenberg's sexuality must always exist in the realm of the potential and the imaginative, for he is incapable of experiencing the actual. In one scene, Urilda, afraid for her father's life, agrees to submit to Wallenberg if he will release Fredolfo, and it is at this moment, when the real intrudes upon his fantasies, that he is impotently helpless and consequently "dashes her from him."

After reading *Fredolfo*, one can understand why it was not well received by its audiences. Maturin, almost as if driven by a demon himself, is uncompromising in his treatment of themes that were usually presented in very veiled terms. At the end of the play, its hero, Adelmar, dies a very unheroic death, and the play's namesake, Fredolfo, is totally scorned by his dying daughter. Maturin has raised heroic possibilities only to dash them to the ground. Toward the beginning of the drama, Maturin seems to be creating the play's hero when Adelmar describes himself as "a child of woe,/ Of persecution, and of mystery," and as a man who "might have been a hero." But Maturin's interests shift—Adelmar is the least successfully realized of all the major characters—and he explores instead the more fascinating subjects of guilt and cruelty in the figures of Berthold and Wallenberg.

Fredolfo was Maturin's last published drama and it is,

in many respects, his best constructed and strongest piece of dramatic writing. His drama is strongest in those scenes in which he can reveal his characters at a moment of heightened emotional intensity either through soliloquy or monologue; but for the most part, Maturin's writing depends upon his creation of mood and of a physical and psychological setting that he could not sufficiently realize within the constraints of drama. He is strongest in his descriptive narrative and in his often detailed analysis of motives and hidden fears and hates, and weakest when writing dialogue. In fiction he was able to use various techniques—letters, manuscripts, diaries, and a fictional narrator—in order to compensate for his weakness in creating credible dialogue. But in spite of the limitations the dramatic form created for Maturin, there are some scenes within *Fredolfo* in which character, action, and language seem perfectly welded together.

But *Fredolfo* must have seemed strong fare to an audience that had been raised on *King Lear* with a happy ending. The stage had seduced Maturin, rewarded him well but briefly for his attentions, and then had unmistakably scorned the gifts with which he presented her. After *Fredolfo's* failure, Maturin resigned himself to the fact that drama was not his medium. He then returned to the writing of fiction for the remaining five years of his life, to the form that had tantalizingly promised him so much and had finally given him so little.

3

The Later Years, 1820–1824

Even at the time of *Fredolfo's* failure, and as early as September 1818, Maturin was already thinking about—if not actually engaged in writing—a new drama and also a romance. The drama, however, was never published and was not produced until six years after Maturin's death. The manuscript of this drama, entitled *Osmyn the Renegade* (also known as *The Siege of Salerno*), had been given to Edmund Kean for his perusal, and he had for unknown reasons refused to return it. Between the years of 1821–1822, it disappeared in London and was not recovered until late in 1825 by William, Maturin's eldest son. It was almost five more years before the play was successfully produced in Dublin. Mrs. Maturin realized 300 pounds from the production, but it was never published and only brief excerpts, quoted by Alaric Watts, have ever appeared in print.

The romance on which Maturin was working was *Melmoth the Wanderer*. He had received from Constable an advance of 500 pounds for *Melmoth* sometime in 1819 and was thus fairly solvent at the time of *Fredolfo's* failure. In August, 1820, *Melmoth* was published, and it remains today the one work for which Maturin is best known. Balzac attested to Maturin's genius and to the greatness of his most famous work by placing Melmoth alongside of Moliere's Don Juan, Goethe's Faust, and Byron's Manfred as one of the four supreme allegorical figures in modern European literature. After reading *Melmoth*, one feels that it was a work that was always within Maturin, waiting for the proper conjunction of time and circumstances to appear. He drew, of course, upon other literary sources, especially Marlowe's Dr. Faustus and Milton's Lucifer; yet *Melmoth* remains wholly Maturin's—his genius and style are indelibly marked throughout it. Using the legend of the Wandering Jew and the legend of Faust, he creates a unique work of art sharing only the broadest and most general similarities with its sources.

Although thematically related to some of Maturin's own writings as well as to the writings of others (for example, Lewis' *The Monk* and Godwin's *St. Leon*), *Melmoth* finally denies comparison and demands that we cope with it on its own terms. And like the fourth book of *Gulliver's Travels*, most of de Sade, and the writings of Celine, the terms established by *Melmoth* are neither easy nor pleasant to recognize or accept. There is no evidence to suggest that Maturin was even remotely insane while writing *Melmoth*; on the contrary, his letters during this period are perfectly lucid and coherent, and his last novel, *The Albigenses*, is certainly not the work of an obsessed or demented mind. Yet, one has the feeling that Maturin, in writing *Melmoth*, calls forth a reality that is so powerful, yet so grotesque, so cruel, and so foreign to Maturin's daily existence, that the dividing line between genius and madness is throughout it very thin. (Indeed, a contemporary account of him during the time he was writing this novel suggests that he was virtually obsessed by his creation.) And Maturin himself frequently alluded to his own creativity in terms of witchcraft—of how he wanted his reader to "sit down by my magic Cauldron, mix my dark ingredients, see the bubbles work, and the spirits rise." The danger, of course, in evoking spirits is that one can never be certain whether he can control them or of the price they will demand from him. The dangers would appear to be multiplied when one calls upon the spirits in their own territory, as Maturin seems to have done in *Melmoth*.

For to write such a novel is to probe those areas of knowledge, both "the visions of another world" and the darkest recesses of the human psyche, which strain the endurance of the mind, and to cross, perhaps irrevocably, forbidden boundaries. The writer then becomes isolated from the world around him, having used the incantatory power of the word to bring forth a reality that borders on the irrational and the insane. He is at once the possessor of secrets he will share with those readers who dare to sit down by his "magic Cauldron" and also possessed by those demons whose presence his art will reveal.

It is possible that Maturin, too, perceived in himself latent traces of insanity or, at least, interests that went beyond what most would call normal, and that he alluded to them in *Melmoth*. In his preface to the 1820 edition, Maturin states that "the original from which the Wife of Walberg is imperfectly sketched is a living woman, and long may she live." The "living woman" is almost certainly Maturin's own wife and the Wife of Walberg is Ines, from "The Tale of Guzman's Family." The tale itself is one of the mildest in *Melmoth*, and the role of Melmoth himself is minimal. The story revolves around Guzman, a wealthy merchant of Seville, whose sister had long ago incurred his wrath by eloping with a German Protestant musician named Walberg. When Guzman thinks that he is about to die, he invites his sister and her family to Seville and establishes them in luxury and wealth, although he refuses to see them. Walberg invites his parents to come from Germany to live with them and for a time, all live happily and comfortably. But when Guzman dies, it is discovered that he has left all of his money to the Church, and so the Walbergs are left penniless. In the midst of poverty and despair, the son sells his blood to a surgeon, the daughter is almost tempted into prostitution, and Walberg becomes virtually insane with worry. During this time, he is visited by Melmoth, but like the others whom Melmoth seeks out, Walberg refuses the terms Melmoth demands in order to help him. Finally the original will, in which Guzman bequeathed all of his money to his sister, is discovered, but not before Walberg almost commits murder. Eventually he recovers from his sickness and the family returns to Germany to live prosperously.

The tale is important for the background and history it gives us of Melmoth, but also for the emotional intensity with which Maturin once again deals with poverty. Like *Manuel*, this part of *Melmoth* is written with such vividness and force of feeling that Maturin's own life shines forth from every page. There are many instances within this story of strong correspondences to Maturin's own experiences—Walberg's feelings of guilt for his inability to provide for his family, his pressing anxieties of how he will get food for them, his squandering of the little money they did have, and his fears of going insane from worry. Most fascinating, however, is the relationship drawn between Walberg and his father. During those times when he himself did not know where the next meal was coming from, Maturin must have, in spite of himself, harbored strong resentment towards his father, who, in his financial ruin, had pulled down his son and his son's family with him. The guilt that this feeling undoubtedly gave rise to seems to be artistically expiated by Maturin in this tale. During one scene in which the family is seated at the dinner table, with barely enough to eat, Walberg grabs some food from his father's hand and gives it to his children, and later, when "the sufferings of his children seemed to inspire him with a kind of wild resentment," Walberg actually raises his arm against his father, "the deaf old man, who was sluggishly devouring his sordid meal." After Walberg recovers from his sickness and finds his father by his side, he is stricken with remorse and begs him for forgiveness. Thus we see Maturin externalizing the agony of his own sufferings, venting his hostilities toward his father, and yet simultaneously expiating his guilt and creating for his tale an ending that he must have hoped would find a parallel in his own life.

But as fascinating as the autobiographical implications of the tale make it, it is but a small part of the novel. *Melmoth* is composed of five tales, the second of which, "The Spaniard's Tale," contains within it the last three tales. In turn, all five tales are contained within a larger frame-story centering around John Melmoth, a descendant of Melmoth the Wanderer. While taking care of a sick uncle during the year 1818, John Melmoth comes across a portrait inscribed "John Melmoth, anno 1646." He is told that the man in the portrait is a distant ancestor who, according to legend, is still alive. John later comes across an old manuscript whose contents form the basis of the first tale, "The Tale of Stanton." The next day, John, while observing a shipwreck on the rocks near the coast, hears a horrible laugh from a man also watching the disaster and recognizes him as the man in the portrait. Frightened, John tries to ascend some rocks, loses his footing, and falls into the water. He awakens in his uncle's house to discover that he has been rescued by the sole survivor of the shipwreck, a Spaniard by the name of Alonzo Moncada. Upon learning John Melmoth's name, Alonzo becomes extremely agitated, and then he tells John the "Tale of the Spaniard." This tale forms all but the few final pages of the novel and contains within itself the "Tale of the Indians," "The Tale of Guzman's Family," and "The Lover's Tale."

Melmoth's structure is tightly organized and possesses an almost geometrical symmetry. The organizational pattern, appropriately described by one critic as resembling a child's set of toy boxes that fit into one another, serves several purposes. First of all, it provides Maturin with a means of maintaining a tight aesthetic control over his material; and, given the nature of the world he creates in *Melmoth*—one filled with cruelty, insanity, torture, and death—such control is imperative. In some respects, *Melmoth* resembles a nightmare contained within a structure that, in its formal preciseness, serves to bring order out of chaos and a strange and haunting beauty out of subjects that are in themselves anything but beautiful. Secondly, the organization makes it possible for Maturin to explore his themes through the techniques of analogy and juxtaposition. For example, Maturin explores the nature of religious persecution in the "Tale of the Spaniard" and the "Tale of the Indians," the nature of love in the "Tale of the Indians" and "The Lover's Tale", and the different aspects of cruelty and insanity in "The Tale of Stanton," the "Tale of the Spaniard," and the "Tale of the Indians." Melmoth's presence in all of the tales creates a continuity by establishing a larger plot structure that links the tales together and by suggesting those common bonds of humanity that exist among characters otherwise separated by both chronology and nationality.

Melmoth's history and character are revealed throughout the novel by persons who have met or heard of him and also by Melmoth's own brief visitations. It is in the "Tale of the Indians" that Melmoth, through his relationship with Immalee, takes on an independent character and importance of his own. Not only does Maturin's technique of gradually revealing Melmoth increase the fear and mystery that surround him, but it is also appropriate that we meet Melmoth in this fashion, since for much of the novel he is primarily an observer, a man who periodically visits persons whom he believes might be willing to exchange their destiny for his own. Not until "The Lover's Tale," the last tale in the novel, do we fully discover the nature of Melmoth's destiny. An Irishman, Melmoth had become attracted to astrology and the occult sciences during a trip to Poland and had been "promised . . . the knowledge and power of the future world—on conditions that are unutterable." Like Faust, Melmoth agreed to give up his soul to diabolic powers in exchange for profound and prophetic knowledge; and he can be released from this pact only if, in the course of 150 years, he can find someone willing to trade places with him. But although his search lasts the full 150 years and takes him to the darkest and most horrible regions of suffering humanity, he is unsuccessful in his quest: "I have traversed the world in the search, and no one, to gain the world, would lose his own soul."

Melmoth is never the immediate cause of suffering—those persons he encounters have suffered not at the hands of some superhuman power, but at the hands of other human beings. In this respect, Melmoth comes to represent those dark truths that men tend to bestow upon a demonic or diabolic world in order to mitigate their own sense of guilt or inadequacy. He is at once apart from and privy to the innermost secrets and hidden deeds of all men; he is a man who has the power to range the earth and to probe the fears and anxieties of other, yet is incapable of gaining power over them or of learning the secrets of his own heart.

What distinguishes Melmoth from Maturin's previous characters is the ambivalence of his emotions and the complex relationship that develops between Melmoth and Immalee. Although at first he views her as a means to escape his destiny he soon falls in love with her; as a consequence, his existence becomes more tormented, yet more beautiful. Immalee, having been raised on an island and knowing only beauty and peace, is an Eve surrounded by depravity, a figure of innocence and beauty in the midst of corruption and evil. By initiating her into the evils of this world, Melmoth buries his own heart deeper in cynicism and despair and thus cuts himself off from the possibilities of redemptive love. Maturin's depiction of the way in which Immalee's innocence and simple faith work upon Melmoth contains some of his very best writing, as he allows Melmoth to rediscover emotions long buried within him. For one brief moment, when he pleads with Immalee to stay, salvation is within his reach, but the moment of reawakening eludes him, and the full implications of it escape that intellect for which he sold his soul.

Immalee does not stay and the secret remains hidden. Love, for Maturin, is redemptive in that it opens the heart to emotions that bring man closer to his fellow beings and to God. Immalee says to Melmoth that "he who is without a God must be without a heart," and the converse of this is also true. He whose heart is closed to love is also separated from God. Like Faust, Melmoth is always within reach of God's salvation, for God's mercy and forgiveness are infinite and require only faith on man's part to be bestowed. His pact with the Devil does not remove Melmoth from God's grace, but his own cynicism and hardness of heart do. Thus his damnation results not from the diabolic powers without, but from within, and in this lies the tragedy of his fate.

For Maturin, most men worship not the Christian God of love and compassion, "the God of smiles and happiness," but a harsh and sadistic deity, "the God of groans and blood." Employing religion as a mask behind which he may enact his basest desires, man perverts the meaning of the worship he engages in and creates a religion of hate and violence. Again in *Melmoth* Maturin explores the ways in which sadism and masochism arise from man's imposition of a system of unnatural and narrow constraints; the Inquisition is a symbol of the institutionalization of such cruelty. Early in their relationship, Melmoth shows Immalee two representative religions—in one flagellation and asceticism are practiced, and in the other torture and persecution. For Maturin, these two expressions of "religion" are inextricably related. The antithesis of Christianity in this novel is represented not by Melmoth, but by a parricide and lay-brother among the ex-Jesuits. His particular theology represents Maturin's final expression of anger and sorrow at what has become of the religion embodied by the Sermon on the Mount: "Mine is the best theology—the theology of utter hostility to all beings whose sufferings may mitigate mine."

Melmoth the Wanderer must be read as a religious work. H. P. Lovecraft in his *Supernatural Horror in Literature*, although critical of *Melmoth's* structure, nevertheless recognizes its religious quality, "a pulse of power undiscoverable in any previous work of this kind—a kinship to the essential truth of human nature, and understanding of the profoundest sources of actual cosmic fear, and a white heat of sympathetic passion on the writer's part. . . ." In *Melmoth*, "Fear is taken out of the realm of the conventional and exalted into a hideous cloud over mankind's very destiny." Dante's Hell has been brought above ground and we see it through the eyes of its inhabitants rather than through the eyes of an observer. At the end, as we hear of Melmoth being pulled down to Hell by demons, the ultimate consequences of cynicism and despair are brought home to bear. In order to present this vision, Maturin had to himself descend more deeply into the Hell within, into the depths of cruelty and horror, and must have been both frightened and fascinated by that curiosity that drove him to write, for example, of two lovers being starved to death in an underground dungeon, or of a man dreaming of being burned alive during an *auto-da-fé*. And although there may be signs of an abnormal imagination in *Melmoth*, such as led reviewers to speak of Maturin as a genius either mad or diabolic, if we try to dismiss such writing too easily, we are reminded, as Maturin wants us to be, of the normal world in which we live, a world in which *autos-da-fé*, wars, Dachau and Auschwitz do exist, a world presided over by normal kings, queens, politicians, and generals. And we are perhaps forced to reconsider our definitions of madness.

Maturin, however far his mind might have traveled into "the dark regions of romance," faced a more immediate and mundane world of unpaid bills and pressing creditors. In 1821, after having lived three years on the 500 pounds he received as an advance for *Melmoth*, he was once again without money, "distrained for taxes," and "under ejectment for rent." It was considerably longer than he anticipated before he published his next, and last, romance, *The Albigenses.* In the meantime, a long blank-verse poem entitled *The Universe* appeared in 1821 with Maturin listed as its author and dedicated to Coleridge "by his sincere admirer, the Author." The poem's authorship became a matter of immediate dispute when a Mr. James Wills claimed that he had written the poem and had been persuaded by Maturin, who had been advanced £500 for a poem he could not finish, to allow him to publish it under his name. It is possible that Maturin had asked Wills to finish the poem—or perhaps even to write all of it—but it is extremely unlikely that he had been advanced such a large sum of money. Whatever the true facts of the controversy are, the poem is at best mediocre and provides no evidence whatsoever of the presence of Maturin's particular genius and talents within it.

The reception of *Melmoth* seems to have driven Maturin into a deeper seclusion and consequently little is known of his public life during his last years. He had succeeded in alienating himself from his Church superiors even before *Melmoth*, had offended the Evangelicals in *Women: or Pour et Contre*, had angered the Catholics in *Melmoth*, and did not even enjoy that compensation of wealth that often accompanies notoriety. His financial situation was worse than it had ever been, and most of his energies were devoted to trying to eke out an existence for himself and his family.

It was not until 1824, the year of his death, that Maturin's last novel, *The Albigenses*, was published. Although it is the longest of Maturin's works, consisting of four volumes and nearly 1500 pages, it was conceived of by him as but the first part of a trilogy "illustrative of European feelings and manners in ancient times, in middle, and in modern." Much has been said of the influence of Scott and the popularity of his historical novels in Maturin's choice of subjects for his last novel. There can be no doubt that Maturin was indebted to Scott and in *The Albigenses* often rendered him through imitation the highest form of honor. But at the same time, it is quite consistent with Maturin's interests that he should have chosen to write a novel focusing on the Middle Ages and, more particularly, on the persecution of the Albigenses. Religious fanaticism, in its many guises, had always fascinated him and the Middle Ages presented him with a rich and often bizarre combination of human experience—of piety existing alongside of superstition, asceticism vying with sensuality, bravery bearing the banner of oppression, and courtly love imposing upon man an unnatural nobility of restraint.

There is, however, a certain ambivalence on Maturin's part towards the material of his last novel. The reason for this ambivalence is that the romantic bent in Maturin—seen in his obvious fondness and sympathy for certain aspects of the feudal ages—is always struggling against an essentially conservative strain within him. On one hand, Maturin is attracted to the age he is describing—to its richness of spirit, to the high ideals it professed, even if it left them too often unpracticed, and to the potential it offered for individual heroism and noble action. This attraction is only partially explained by the fact that Maturin was contemporary with the rise of romanticism and its interest in the literature and culture of other ages. More important in Maturin's case is the temperamental affinities he had with whatever partook of the aristocratic, an affinity seen in the legends Maturin used to tell of his own family's noble origins.

But if Maturin was politically and emotionally attracted to certain aspects of the Middle Ages, his philosophical and theological view of man prevented him from writing a conventional romance of history extolling the nobility of the age. Maturin might show affinities with the romantic temperament in his belief in nature's salutary powers and in its capacity to provide man with a glimpse of his Creator; but he does not share the romantic's belief in the innate goodness of man or in man's unlimited potential for social and ethical improvement. Goodness and even nobility are possible, although rare, but are constantly endangered by the forces of chance and mutability as well as by man's own propensity toward the base and the ignoble. For Maturin man's struggle toward the noble and the good is fraught with additional danger by the fact that such a struggle often represses those human desires that if denied for long will ultimately turn against man and destroy him.

His idealization of the age, however, does come through in his depiction of women in *The Albigenses*. In *Women* and *Melmoth*, Zaira, Eva, and Immalee stand among the most memorable of his characters; in *The Albigenses*, on the other hand, Maturin creates two women who, in their conventionality of thought and action, closely resemble those typical romantic heroines he earlier satirized in a review of Radcliffe's novels. In the case of Genevieve, the granddaughter of the aged leader of the Albigenses, Maturin apparently envisioned every possible trial and tribulation that a heroine could face and then created circumstances whereby she could experience them all. She is sent into exile for rendering aid to a wounded knight she eventually marries, saves a group of women from being assaulted, is almost seduced by the Bishop of Toulouse, saves the life of Queen Ingelberg, and soon must use this fact to protect herself from the dishonourable advances of the Queen's son, the Dauphin of France. As if this were not enough adventure for a girl not yet twenty years old, she also meets and talks with Eloise, the immortal lover of Abelard. Isabelle, the other heroine, has fewer adventures—she falls in love with and marries a young knight whose destiny it is to kill the last survivor of the Courtenaye family: Isabelle herself. But through the aid of what is perhaps Maturin's strangest combination of protagonists, a Catholic monk and a sorceress, this disaster is averted and toward the end of the novel, a double wedding takes place.

If *The Albigenses* consisted only of the perils and plights of its two heroes and two heroines, it would be in no way distinguished from the many historical romances tha were flooding the market in Maturin's time, most of them trying to capitalize on Scott's success. Fortunately there is much more than that. First of all, Maturin provides us with a vast and sweeping panoramic view of the historical and religious background. He is also quite successful in capturing the essence of the age's most important figures. Both Simon de Montfort and the Bishop of Toulouse come across larger than life—in their energy and strength, in their enjoyment of the power they wielded, in their mutual hatred of the Albigenses, and in the struggle waged between them to gain recognition as the Champion of the Church. Because Maturin draws them with such vividness, he forces the reader to share his ambivalent attitude toward them. Even though we recognize their cruelty, their boundless egotism, and the discrepancy between their actions and the religion they are professedly defending, we are begrudgingly forced to give them at least our qualified admiration.

If Maturin's historical interests and his romantic impulses are responsible for his creation of those larger-than-life characters, there is another recurrent impulse in Maturin that checks his admiration for the Middle Ages. He is aware that even his most heroic figures were driven, in part, by unheroic needs and desires; like *Women* and, to a lesser extent, *Melmoth*, *The Albigenses* is a study of religious fanaticism. For Maturin, fanaticism under any guise separates man from himself and from his fellowmen; religious fanaticism, however, is especially dangerous because it deadens one to the feelings of sympathy and compassion and because the energy and enthusiasm of religious fervor are often turned, through violence, hatred, and rigid moral certainty, against religion itself. If Maturin had angered the Evangelicals in *Women*, the Catholics in *Melmoth*, in this novel he succeeded in antagonizing them both. But we have to believe Maturin (in spite of his fantasizing about the sexual and sadistic propensities of Catholic priests) when he maintains that he was not criticizing religion, but rather the perversion of religion by those "who . . . painted heaven to their imaginations and their hearers as a place whose joys would be exalted by their consciousness of the interminable sufferings of their persecutors and enemies."

The fact remains, however, that Maturin became progressively more alienated—at least in his fiction—from all organized religion, namely because he felt that any religion that tries to impose its will or creed upon others is in danger of transforming what should be an order of joy and love into an order of suffering and hatred. It is not simply coincidental that the two religious leaders who most clearly represent Maturin's ideal of the religious man, Pierre, the leader of the Albigenses, and the Monk of Montcalm, both antagonize the power structures of their respective churches. Maturin's ultimate distrust of all formal religion is further seen in the fact that the novel's true moral center is found in a scene reminiscent of Voltaire—a writer with whom Maturin shared more than he would have admitted—and involves a shepherd totally isolated from the outside world of chivalry, politics, and religious wars. Professing to a very simple and almost pagan religion, the shepherd is harshly chastized by visitors for his backwardness and informed of the ways of the civilized world beyond, where religion is such an important issue that it "had been the cause of wars that had desolated the fairest provinces of France; that it had marshalled armies with princes and pontiffs at their head; and already cost the lives of thirty thousand men, sacrificed by their own countrymen. . . . " But the shepherd, preferring his own ways, decided to remain uncivilized and "as the first light of dawn gleamed through the crevice, he unbarred his door, and silently motioned his guests to depart."

There are many strengths in *The Albigenses*—Maturin's imaginative recreating of the crusade of the Catholic Church against the Albigenses, his characterization of those men on both sides who play crucial roles in the campaign, and his probing of those emotions and often unacknowledged desires that were concealed beneath the banners of religion and chivalry—but in spite of this, Maturin's genius, that force we feel on virtually every page of *Melmoth*, is only sporadically present. This novel is finally weakened by the fact that Maturin is always so evidently in control of it. He knew too well those talents he possessed for creating an exciting tale and for peopling it with tormented characters; and in *The Albigenses* these skills appear, but in a tired and imitative fashion, lacking the imaginative force and capacity to court the unknown and horrible possessed by *Melmoth*.

It is, of course, impossible to foresee what Maturin would have written had he lived to complete his trilogy, but he seems to lack both the energy and the desire to bring his project to a conclusion, and Maturin lived on after *Melmoth* in poverty and isolation, fulfilling in life the debilitating and oppressive fate of those poverty-ridden and tormented characters about whom he wrote with such apprehension. On October 30, 1824 Charles Robert Maturin died at the age of forty-four. As his health faded in the last months of his life, he became even more isolated and consequently very little is known of this time. It was apparently a time of great depression for him, compounded by the anxieties of poverty and by illness exacerbated by long hours of work and little sleep during his composition of *The Albigenses*. Shortly after Maturin's death, his wife wrote to Scott:

> You no doubt by this time are acquainted with the death of my dear departed husband; he has left me with four children, the youngest of whom is only five years old, totally unprovided for—he laboured with incessant assiduity for his family even after it had pleased the Almighty to deprive him of health—his sufferings with regard to pecuniary circumstances preyed on a constitution naturally delicate, till at last it put a period to his existence—

Scott had planned to visit Maturin in the summer of 1825, but Maturin died before he could meet the man who had for twelve years advised, consoled and encouraged him, and on several occasions had provided the only money that stood between Maturin and starvation.

After Maturin's death, two rumors circulated, both of which are false. The first was that Maturin's eldest son, William, had burned all of his father's manuscripts because of the shame he felt in his father's connection with the stage. William's letters to Scott after his father's death completely refute this rumor and suggest that he made every effort to have his father's literary remains either produced on stage or published. The second rumor—that Maturin had consciously precipitated his own death through a mistake in his medicines—is the sort of story that Maturin's eccentric habits and behavior would encourage, but it too, as Idman suggests, is unfounded. James Clarence Mangan, who knew Maturin during those final years, recalls seeing him shortly after he had officiated at a funeral:

> His long pale, melancholy, Don Quixote, out-of-the-world face would have inclined you to believe that Dante, Bajazet, and the Cid had risen together from their sepulchres, and clubbed their features for the production of an effect. But. . . . The great Irishman, like Hamlet, had that within him which passed show, . . . He bore the 'thunder-scars' about him, but they were graven, not on his brow, but on his heart.

The comparison of Maturin to Hamlet need not be examined, but Mangan's allusions to Dante and Don Quixote are relevant in considering Maturin's life and art. The romantic poets had explored that "deep and romantic chasm," that "savage place" Coleridge writes of in "Kubla Khan," but had pulled up short, except for the later books of *Don Juan*, in their description of what they found. The gothic novelists had, on the other hand, written of the emotions of fear and terror, but had relied heavily on external machinery and on a topography of horror often used for its own sake. Maturin's contribution to British literature is found in his ability to synthesize these two traditions, taking the literary medium provided by the gothic novel, but using it to examine more deeply those aspects of human experience embodied in those figures, such as Faust and the Wandering Jew, that had captured the romantic imagination. Yet Maturin is cut off from those romantics who preceded him by a strong Calvinistic vein that finally prevented him, in spite of his own romantic leanings, from seeking redemption, or even solace from love, be it of Man, nature, or God. Few of the love relationships that he depicts are successful and even fewer of his novels end happily.

In one respect *Melmoth* is Maturin's attempt to find a basis for hope and belief; and in so far as none of the persons confronted by Melmoth is willing to sell his soul for worldly happiness, Maturin's world differs from Dante's Hell in the all-important fact that hope has not been abandoned. Immalee is the embodiment of Melmoth's antithesis: in her joy, beauty, and innocence we see Man as he once was and as Maturin would like to be; but she too is fated to die in an Inquisition dungeon, isolated and estranged from all but God.

Because Maturin's world is in many ways monstrous and cruel, his influence was felt most strongly not among the Victorian novelists, but among the French romantics, who found in Edgar Allen Poe and Maturin kindred investigators of that monstrous landscape Baudelaire was to traverse in *Les Fleurs du Mal*. Some of the later nineteenth-century British writers, such as Rossetti and Oscar Wilde, were to speak highly of Maturin, and one can see in *The Picture of Dorian Gray* why Wilde might have been attracted to the writings of his fellow countryman. In fact, during Wilde's final days of exile in Paris, after his release from prison, he assumed the name of "Sebastian Melmoth."

If Maturin's works evoke in their probing of the diabolic an image of Dante's *Inferno*, his own life in some respects painfully reminds one of Don Quixote. There was a certain naiveté and innocence about Maturin that worked against him in his quest for success, and he was unable to understand how his literature could possibly offend his superiors in the church. He maintained an unrealistic expectation that wise and rational men would and could keep separate the content of a novel from the moral character of the man who wrote it. To the very end of his painful life, he kept the hope, against all reason, that some person or event would intervene to alleviate his distress. One can only wish that Maturin had had his own Sancho Panza, someone who was as familiar with the realities of this world as Maturin was with the realities of the other world.

But Maturin is neither English, Italian, nor Spanish; he is Irish, and his work must finally be judged in terms of the Irish tradition. He has, of course, no place in that tradition if one excludes from his study all writers except the "Irish-speaking Irish." Maturin is an Anglo-Irishman who wrote in English primarily for an English audience; and although according to Thomas Flanagan's *The Irish Novelists*, 1800–1850, he and Lefanu are outside the mainstream of even this tradition because they "turned to tales whose somber and uncanny atmosphere seeks to transcend the immediacies of social fact," it is difficult to speak of Maturin as other than an Irish novelist, if only by virtue of the problems he shared in common with other Irish writers of his time. He faced the problems of trying to define Ireland as he saw it for a people who viewed it for the most part as an alien culture. Throughout his writings, and especially in *The Wild Irish Boy* and *The Milesian Chief*, he wrestles not only with the problem of Ireland's identity but also tries to educate his reading audience in Ireland's history, her traditions, her strengths, and her weaknesses. Maturin's love for Ireland shapes what he wrote and is manifest in the characters he created, from his aged chiefs to his blind and prophetic bards, in the Irish myths, music, and poetry that he spoke of, and in his descriptions of Ireland's lanscape and cities. He was, however, as firmly rooted in the present political and economic realities of Ireland as he was steeped in Irish folklore and history. As an Irish Protestant with Tory political leanings, he did not believe that Ireland could exist independently of England, but he writes, not as a political theorist or pamphleteer, but as a novelist, and his writings provide us not with answers, but with the articulation of problems. In the problems he writes of and in the conflict between his heart and head where the question of Ireland is concerned, we can see his sense of personal estrangement as an Irishman, and this estrangement is reflected in many of his major Irish characters who are drawn by the past but must find their role in the present.

Maturin was the author of six novels and three published plays; yet he is remembered today, if at all, only for *Melmoth the Wanderer*. It is unlikely that there will be a resurgence of interest in Maturin in the near future, even though at least two of his novels, *The Milesian Chief* and *Women: or Pour et Contre*, definitely do not deserve the obscurity they have suffered. But it is fitting that history has chosen to remember Maturin for that strange and foreboding Wanderer, for in Melmoth Maturin created, with fear and fascination, a figure who embodies in his isolation, his wanderings, and his descent into the recesses of the human heart, those haunted and darkened passages of his own genius. Through the magic of the written word, he evoked demons from within the human mind, and they, in turn, retaliated upon their summoner by isolating and estranging him from that world into which they were called. Of Maturin, James Clarence Mangan wrote:

> He—in his own dark way—understood many people; but nobody understood him in *any* way. And therefore it was that he, this man of the highest genius, Charles Robert Maturin, lived unappreciated—and died unsympathized with, uncared for, unenquired after—and not only forgotten, because he had never been thought about.

We may hope that his insights are not proved by history to be as prophetic as they are sensitive.

Selected Bibliography

THE PRINCIPAL WORKS OF CHARLES ROBERT MATURIN

(Dates refer to the first editions, unless otherwise noted)

Drama:

Bertram; or the Castle of St. Aldobrand. London: John Murray, 1816.

Manuel. London: John Murray, 1817.

Fredolfo. London: Constable and Co., 1819.

Fiction:

The Family of Montorio; or the Fatal Revenge. 3 vols. London: Longman, Hurst, Rees, and Orme, 1807.

The Wild Irish Boy. 3 vols. London: Longman, Hurst, Rees, and Orme, 1808.

The Milesian Chief. 4 vols. London: Henry Colburn, 1812.

Women; or Pour et Contre. 3 vols. Edinburgh: Constable and Co., 1818.

Melmoth the Wanderer. 4 vols. Edinburgh: Constable and Co., 1820. There is also a recent edition of this novel, edited and introduced by William F. Axton, Lincoln: Univ. of Nebraska, 1961.

The Albigenses. 4 vols. London: Hurst, Robinson and Co., 1824.

Letters:

The Correspondence of Sir Walter Scott and Charles Robert Maturin, ed.

and intro. by Fannie E. Ratchford and Wm. H. McCarthy, Jr., Austin: Univ. of Texas, 1937.

SECONDARY STUDIES

Melmoth the Wanderer. vol. 1. London: Richard Bentley and Son, 1892. This particular edition, in addition to containing as its frontispiece the famous Brocas portrait of Maturin, also possesses some valuable biographical and bibliographical information: 1) "Memoirs of Charles Robert Maturin"; 2) "Separate Notices of Each Book"; 3) "A Note on Charles Robert Maturin"; 4) "A List of Works by Charles Robert Maturin, With Translations and Adaptations by Other Authors."

Axton, William F. "Introduction," *Melmoth the Wanderer*. Lincoln: University of Nebraska, 1961.

Hume, Robert D. "Gothic Versus Romantic: A Revaluation of the Gothic Novel," *PMLA*, 84 (1969), 282–290.

Idman, Nilo. *Charles Robert Maturin: His Life and Works*. London: Constable and Co., 1923. A pioneering study containing a valuable bibliography.

Lovecraft, H. P. *Supernatural Horror in Literature*. New York: Ben Abramson, 1945.

Railo, Eino. *The Haunted Castle: A Study of the Elements of English Romanticism*. London: George Routledge and Sons, 1927.

Scholten, Willem. *Charles Robert Maturin: The Terror-Novelist*. Amsterdam: H. J. Paris, 1933.

Varma, Devendra P. *The Gothic Flame*. New York: Russel and Russel, 1957.